The ITS Professional Job Changing System

*Our client handbook... a guide
to what we will be doing for you...
the service we will be providing...
and some key things you should know*

by Bob Gerberg

National Center & Headquarters
7979 East Tufts Avenue
Denver, CO 80237
866-328-2685 • Fax 888-559-0883
On the web at: www.itspersonalmarketing.com

The journey you are undertaking with our firm.

Envision for a moment, that you're about to accomplish a much better career move... and probably more than you ever imagined was possible.

With our state-of-the-art service and the resources we put behind you, there will be little that can stop your success. As you will see in this handbook, you will have the advantage of everything that's possible today... being done to support your move.

For over 98% of our clients... all that's required is their commitment and their motivation... along with a willingness to become an expert on the subject of personal marketing. There's nothing technical about doing that... it's just a matter of giving your career search the priority it deserves.

Each year, thousands of our clients tell us that they have begun new jobs, that at one time they would not have thought possible. Many tell us that they have achieved a long list of personal goals... including the majority of the things most of our clients list on page 43.

They include greater income, more responsibility, more recognition, a better future, an enjoyable new environment, less travel, getting into a new industry, joining a growth company or a firm that is #1 in its field... and other factors. Making you successful is how we grow our firm.

Introduction

Services in advance of your search

Searching & getting interviews

Interviewing & negotiating

Reference

ABOUT THE AUTHOR

Bob Gerberg is among America's foremost authorities on every aspect of professional job hunting. More than 10 million copies of books and programs he has created are in circulation.

His ideas have been instrumental in helping millions throughout the world who have looked for new positions. Over more than 25 years he has authored dozens of books and audio cassettes.

These include publications such as *The Professional Job Hunter's Guide, The Professional Job Changing System, An Easier Way to Change Jobs, Sixty Great Letters Which Won New Jobs, $100,000 and Above—The New Realities of Executive Job Hunting, 15 New Rules for Job Hunting Success* and others.

He has also written numerous articles and complete job hunting programs. These include *The Career Advancement Series*... a package of 28 small booklets on vital job hunting subjects.

He has also authored programs that have consisted of 6 to 16 audio cassettes... supplemented by 8 specialty publications. These include *TAPIT, The Personal Marketing Program, The Executive Job Changing System* and others. Over the years, hundreds of thousands of these programs have been used in outplacement programs by institutions ranging from the U.S. Marine Corps and the CIA through major universities, associations and numerous Fortune 1000 corporations.

Initially with GE, after his service as a U.S. Air Force officer, Bob's early career was with Honeywell and major food companies including PepsiCo and a major supermarket chain. He held positions as Director of Marketing Research, Director of New Products, and VP Marketing Services and Assistant to the Chairman of a Fortune 500 firm.

Active in the career field for over two decades, he licensed a system for executive job search to independent career firms worldwide... from 1987 to 1997.

With the emergence of the Internet, he formulated the architecture for the new ITS approach to finding positions and the firm is now America's leading provider of job changing resources. Each year, the firm helps thousands of professionals to achieve their career goals.

Mr. Gerberg has a B.A. from Colgate University, a year of studies sponsored by the United States Air Force, an M.B.A. from the University of Pittsburgh and advanced executive studies at MIT, sponsored by PepsiCo. A resident of New York and New Jersey for most of his career, he and his wife Joan now reside in Denver, Colorado.

WHY JOB HUNTING IS A CHALLENGE

For the past 20 years, the time it takes to find a good new position—*has grown longer*. Here's what others say about this. First, you may be surprised to know that the *U.S. Labor Department* has said it takes the average professional... from start to finish... 6 to 12 months to find a job.

Second, *Fortune Magazine* did a cover story a few years ago... entitled "Over 40 and Out of Work." It talked about the difficult journey people face... and the strain, confusion and worry that is often involved.

More recently, *The Chicago Tribune* had an article commenting on the problems facing people after age 50. A survey of people who lost their jobs... indicated that only 5%... or 1 in 20... are able to get back to their previous level of income and responsibility.

The New York Times voiced a similar concern... claiming that unemployment statistics are misleading. 9 million professionals are no longer on the unemployment rolls... but are essentially underemployed in lower positions, the only jobs they could win.

When you look for a job, the most important thing is to have the right contacts... or to access the right openings. But... most people don't have connections... or can't find enough good openings.

Job hunting to many people is just answering ads... contacting some recruiters and networking friends. Some post their resume on a few job boards. This is all that millions of people do. Of course, anyone who relies on these limited actions will uncover only a fraction of the good situations out there.

Why are there so many people in the market? Because of financial pressures, employers routinely go through staff reductions when sales decline. This has led to sharply declining employee loyalty.

Now, instead of looking for a job every 7 years... people change jobs on an average of once every 4 years. This alone has doubled the level of competition. People are also living and working longer. Further complications stem from the emergence of the Internet as a national exchange place for resumes.

Of particular importance are the job boards. Many people now leave their resumes posted online—even after they accept new positions. So, in today's job market, we have both active and passive job seekers. One job board claims that almost 60 million resumes are in their database—which they sell to employers as a recruiting tool.

HOW YOU CAN AVOID THESE CHALLENGES

To succeed in a job search today, you must first have an understanding of the new job market and how it works. You will quickly *have this.* You will also need to get connected to the openings and leads you require... which *we will supply.*

But today, you also face an additional challenge. To be effective, you need to communicate through multiple resumes as well as letters, emails and conversations. Marketing yourself is not simple. That's why *we will create your materials for you.*

At the same time, you must get your credentials into play on a large enough scale, and cut through the clutter that exists because of millions of other resumes. Again, we will play a major role here as *we get your materials placed* with key recruiters, growth firms, major employers and perhaps venture capitalists.

Given today's competitive climate, the key thing you need to do is to give your career search the priority it deserves with respect to other things in your life, especially with a lot at stake. This is why your career advancement should be given priority at this time.

The goal of this client handbook is to cement your understanding of a number of basic things. They won't all be relevant to your situation, but if you follow the ones that are — your confidence will soar and you'll be on your way.

SOME INITIAL COMMENTS

On industry change & growth firms

Changes in the past were made by luck or circumstance. Today changing industries can be under your control. Growth industries and fast growing firms are where the action is… and there is often far less competition.

On being unemployed

A common perception is that employers feel that good talent doesn't last long in the market. So, get into action—fast.

On age barriers

Age is not the barrier that you may think. Veteran talent is always valued. Google, Sony and Apple all made news last year when they hired people in their 50s and 60s. The key is marketing yourself in the right way.

On getting market coverage

You want maximum exposure when you are in the market. Why settle for 2% when technology can make 85% available? Job hunting the old way means experiencing months of trial and error and frustration.

On being aggressive

Here's the benefit in a nutshell. If you had a valuable piece of art to auction, would you prefer 15 or 25 bidders, or just 1 or 2?

On old resume formulas
They no longer work... because of the volume of resumes which are now faxed or emailed—or simply left posted online.

On recruiters and venture capitalists
For people with good tickets, placing a significant number of resumes with recruiters and venture capitalists (VCs) can be very productive.

On creating your own job
The more senior you are, the more likely your next position will be created for you.

On contacting employers directly
Increasingly, hiring at all levels is database driven. Getting your credentials to a lot of key employers as well as recruiters is crucial.

On privacy issues and the Internet
Improperly revealing details can haunt you for many years—because of resume scanning. Identity theft is a growing problem because of too much disclosure over the Internet.

On knowing how to negotiate
Many people get initial offers raised by 10% to 30%... and some get signing bonuses from $7,500 to $100,000. With our resources behind you, why not set some high goals.

THINGS YOU SHOULD KNOW ABOUT US & WHO WE ARE

About 8 years ago, a group of seasoned professionals founded the *ITS* firm. They shared an interest in developing a significant breakthrough in the job hunting field.

The firm initially focused on selling outplacement services. Clients we served included *Citigroup, Eaton, Ingersoll, Johnson Controls, Kellogg, Novartis, Sun Microsystems,* and many others.

At that time, we assisted corporate officers and former entrepreneurs... people earning from *$150,000 to over $1 million.* Today, besides working for executives, we now serve professionals seeking from *$50,000 to $150,000...* people motivated by challenge, greater career enjoyment, future opportunity and equity. These people often seek financial growth and know it's important to be in the right industry.

We have also helped people outside business... including celebrities, athletes leaving professional sports, mid-level and senior military, professionals leaving their own businesses and many others.

The firm maintains a national center with regional offices across the U.S. Our staff of approximately 300 includes a wealth of experienced professionals including former CEOs, CFOs, marketing executives, attorneys, educators, HR professionals and many other talented professionals.

Some of our partners/shareholders are on the pages that follow. You can visit all of them on our company website at www.itspersonalmarketing.com.

ITS

- Our shareholders are employees.
- Many have 20 years' experience.
- We have handled 30,000 campaigns.
- We have $30 million invested.
- We are the leaders in our field.
- We are selective in accepting clients.
- All clients must be marketable.
- All clients must be committed.
- Our staff is highly committed.
- We reinvest and change quarterly.
- Our client base is worldwide.

WHEN IS THE RIGHT TIME TO LAUNCH YOUR SEARCH?

Many people concern themselves about the job market. But, what makes national news about the market will have little to do with the reception you have in the marketplace. In good economies or bad, every year the total number of employed Americans increases.

Another key thing to keep in mind is that people do have certain career situations that can get worse. The longer you wait, the worse a situation may become.

The longer a person remains on the brink of losing a job, unhappy every day, under stress or unchallenged, the deeper the hole that person may dig for themselves. If you wait and allow this to happen, the negative impact on your mental outlook can be severe. You will never be able to approach marketing yourself with the right frame of mind.

Some liabilities also get worse with time. If you have topped out, or stayed in one industry or firm for a long time, you will get increasingly less marketable. Of course, age clearly gets more challenging with time. Things will only be more serious later on.

You also need to concern yourself with your achievements that may have been significant, but which can lose their impact as time goes on.

You must give your search a priority in your life. Many people remain in negative situations too long and their marketability declines.

WHAT WE'LL DO FOR YOU THAT NO ONE ELSE DOES

- We write 3 superior resumes... and draft 12 letters.
- We enable you to access almost all published openings.
- We supply continuous leads to emerging situations.
- We place your credentials with recruiters and employers.
- You will have continuous 24/7 research support.
- We back you with continuous team support.
- Our staff assists throughout interviews & negotiations.
- If you have issues or concerns that might restrict you... we will develop solutions based on our experience.
- If you want to explore new industries, we will help identify some new industry options that may be right.

The team we put behind you

- A marketing director is your main contact.
- Our research staff is available.
- Our Internet staff is available.
- A client services specialist will contact you.
- Our negotiation specialists are also available.

Our searches are more successful than what people can achieve on their own. We follow a classic business principle. An organized team working full time and with access to the right resources, will invariably outperform an individual operating on his or her own.

1 We will enable you to compete in all 8 segments of today's job market.

All market segments are avenues to opportunities. To help you we supply the vast majority of all openings that become public. We also supply leads to emerging opportunities. And, we also aggressively market your credentials to recruiters, growth firms, and large employers.

The Published Job Market
(average for all income levels)

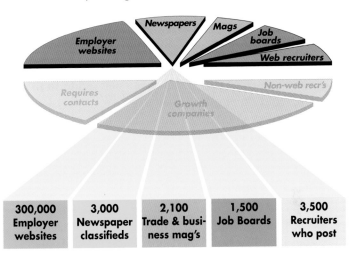

300,000 Employer websites	3,000 Newspaper classifieds	2,100 Trade & business mag's	1,500 Job Boards	3,500 Recruiters who post

The Unpublished Job Market
(average for all income levels)

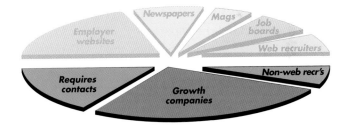

**See page 36 for the breakdown
of the market at your income level**

THE PUBLISHED MARKET

When employers decide to hire someone... there is an event that leads to their decision. Typically, someone has quit or been separated. Turnover leads to over 95% of all jobs opening up.

Now once that decision has been made to fill a job, what do employers do first? Well, they look within their company... and they look at candidates on file in their recruiting database. That's why we place our client's credentials with their best prospects. We want their names to come up when a job opens up.

If they can't fill a job, what do employers do next? This is where the top half of the pie chart comes in... "the published job market." This is also where 99% of all job hunters compete. The bottom half is "the unpublished job market."

Let's first talk about the published openings and the employer websites. Over 300,000 employers now post their openings. We track the 100,000 major employers who now recruit this way. Openings in 3,000 newspapers, 2,100 magazines and over 1,500 job boards come next. Of course, Monster, Career Builder and Hot Jobs are best known, but there are many others out there that might help you.

On the pie chart on the last page, you'll also see web recruiters. About 3,500 post openings. As we'll cover later, ITS can put virtually all of the published openings at your fingertips. Many can then respond to 20 times more situations.

THE UNPUBLISHED MARKET

The bottom half of the chart is "the unpublished market." One part is the "non-web" recruiters who keep openings private. Here, you need to place a superior resume. At ITS, we do this for you. Some recruiters may call right away. Others may call throughout a search as something comes up.

Right next to non-web recruiters are the growth companies. This is where the action is in the job market. These firms are constantly hiring. They often offer strong financial packages... and because they are growing so fast, previous industry experience rarely matters. Transferable skills do!

With this in mind, ITS tracks growth industries and growth companies... over 10,000 of them, and we often place client resumes with these firms.

Now, for the part of the market that "requires contacts"... if you don't have connections... or cannot network your way in, how do you compete? There are two ways. One is to get "leads" to these jobs—something we will do for you... as we will cover later. The other is to place a strong statement of your credentials with "high probability" employers. We will also do this for you.

In addition to requests for interviews, these placements often produce a continuous flow of new contacts which offer networking opportunities.

By the way, when you get interviews for jobs in the unpublished segment... how much less competition will you encounter? The answer is... a lot less!

The Job Market—If You Are Seeking $101K to $150K

Jobs at this income level are 25% published and 75% unpublished. This is in stark contrast to the market in total for all income levels. Even with only 25% published, there will be many openings made publicly available, but they draw the highest numbers of applicants... often into the hundreds.

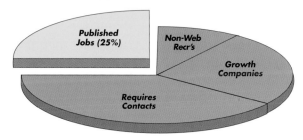

75% Unpublished

The Job Market—If You Are Seeking $150K to $200K

Available jobs in this income range are still only 10% published and 90% unpublished. At this level the majority of firms are still reluctant to place these openings on their websites, although exceptions exist among some major firms. Newspapers and magazines are playing a much smaller role here and the published openings that appear on Internet job boards are greatly exaggerated... as many are repeated and remain on different sites long after they are filled.

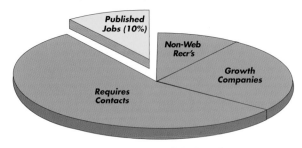

90% Unpublished

The Job Market—If You Are Seeking $200K and Above

Despite the growth of the Internet, the top executive jobs available are predominantly unpublished. The one exception is in the nonprofit and education sectors where positions are more often published in specialized media and sometimes in trade and high circulation publications. The total number of jobs available in any week at this level are extremely limited, and anyone who is serious about maximizing their market exposure must take advantage of all possibilities for getting access to available positions which are unpublished. At this level, the rewards go to those who are most aggressive in placing superior statements of their credentials.

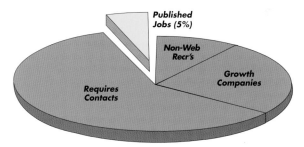

95% Unpublished

Note: These job market projections are within a reasonable accuracy. The ITS research staff has the advantage through our subsidiary JMAC, of having technology which allows us to capture virtually all openings that ever appear on the Internet... along with links to all newspapers and trade magazines. We combined our data with that available from various sources of the staffing industry. This industry is generally estimated to be a $50 billion+ industry and includes all temp agencies, employment agencies, contingency and retainer based executive recruiters, and all outplacement and career transition firms.

JOBS AT YOUR INCOME LEVEL

There are 145 million people employed in the U.S. Of these, 3% report income above $150,000. That means 4.3 million jobs exist at this income and above. But on average, they open up only once every 4 years... because this is how often people change jobs.

So, in any given week, there are about 21,000 jobs available at this income level. *But these are spread among all 50 states, over 200 industries... and all occupations! This means that, when executives look for a job at $150,000 or $250,000 or more... what are their chances?*

How many jobs are out there in the locations where they are... in their career field... and their industries of interest? Very few at any one moment.

There are similar challenges at levels from $60,000 to $100,000... and $100,000 to $150,000. Again, the problem is that the jobs are in all 50 states, 200+ industries and in all professions.

The bottom line is that there are a lot fewer jobs out there than most people think, and finding them and getting considered can be a major challenge.

Again, there are contributing factors. The Internet attracts millions to the same popular websites... causing 200 or 300 people to apply for the same opening. Yet, the "bad" little secret of the Internet is that many of the published jobs... are repeated 10 and 12 times at different websites... and listed long after the jobs are filled. The following pages will review some statistics that may interest you.

U.S. EMPLOYMENT—145 MILLION

When most people look for a job, they are unaware of the income scale in the U.S.... and where they currently fit.

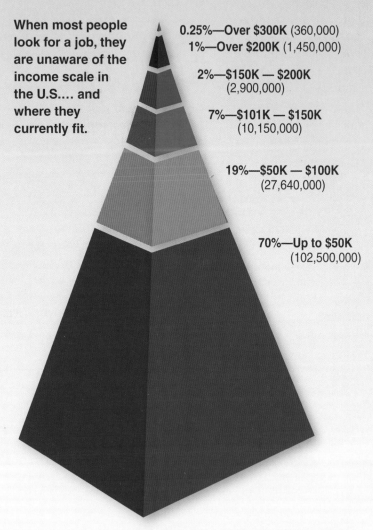

0.25%—Over $300K (360,000)
1%—Over $200K (1,450,000)

2%—$150K — $200K
(2,900,000)

7%—$101K — $150K
(10,150,000)

19%—$50K — $100K
(27,640,000)

70%—Up to $50K
(102,500,000)

* Data on this page and the following pages from staffing industry projections, the IRS and the U.S. Labor Department.

U.S. JOBS AVAILABLE—EACH WEEK

The last chart shows total jobs by income. The Labor Department says professional/executive jobs open up once every 4 years. When you divide by 208 weeks… you can identify the number that become open each week. As they open, an equal amount get filled. Essentially this is the U.S. job market.

The actual market in any given income range is much smaller than most people realize. What counts is the number of jobs available in any given week.

	Ea. week	During ea. month
Over $300K	2,100	9,100
Over $200K	7,000	30,000
Between $150K & $200K	14,000	60,000
Between $101K & $150K	49,000	212,000
Between $50K & $100K	132,000	572,000

PUBLISHED VS. UNPUBLISHED JOBS

As you go up in income, a lower percentage of jobs are released to the published market. The vast majority of all positions under $50,000 are now published. That means that they appear on employer websites... or in 2,100 leading newspapers... the 3,500 leading trade magazines... the 1,500 job boards... and on the websites of the 3,500 recruiters that list their openings for the public to review. For positions at higher incomes, it becomes essential to uncover... and be considered for... unpublished openings.

	Published jobs	Unpublished jobs
Over $200K	5%	95%
Between $150K & $200K	10%	90%
Between $101K & $150K	25%	75%
Between $50K & $100K	50%	50%
Up to $50K	90%	10%

The 3 ways to unpublished jobs

Have contacts & network

Get leads to emerging jobs

Have your credentials placed

■ We help get you contacts

■ We supply you with continuous leads

■ We place your credentials with high probability prospects

It's important to understand that hiring in the U.S. has become increasingly database driven.
Most segments of the market are now database driven. To compete for more than just the positions that come on the published market in any given week, you need to get into the databases of the job boards and employer websites.

To compete for unpublished jobs, you also need to get into the databases of as many recruiters as possible. This includes all growth firms and key employers who might be good prospects for you... now and in the future. Venture capitalists operate the same way... turning to their files of candidates when a need to hire occurs.

When you are in the databases of a wide range of organizations, you will essentially be competing for the jobs that open up every week... *not just in one week!* When something comes on the market that you are a good fit for... you get calls. Of course, this is another reason why your materials have to be the very best they can be.

Besides what you surface now, the benefits can accrue for years.

2 Our first step is to help make sure you pursue the right job hunting goals.

When you complete our profiles, ITS will surface all of your experiences and transferable skills in an organized way. This is supplemented by our teleconference discussions. Then, we will jointly decide on the right goals.

WE WILL JOINTLY DETERMINE
THE RIGHT GOALS FOR YOU

It may surprise you, but many people pursue the wrong job titles. However, if their transferable skills are clarified, they can be repositioned for different goals, and sometimes for much more advancement than they thought possible.

We all have seen career fields change dramatically over a decade. Fields that once offered great opportunity have become financially confining with limited growth possibilities.

Does print advertising offer the same career possibilities as it did a decade ago? Does selling in the steel industry? Does manufacturing management in textiles? Career fields change at a much faster pace than most people realize.

We don't want you to take a narrow view of yourself, because we've seen that lead to mistakes. For example, if you see yourself as a specialist (i.e., a banker), you may believe you are locked into a given career. Believe it or not, there are 23,000 different job titles in use today, but 95% of all professionals fall within one of several hundred career specialties which are usually in significant demand.

So, it is important for us to jointly decide on exactly what you should go after. Of course, you'll dramatically improve your chances by pursuing titles that the market makes available in abundance.

While you are thinking about goals… here are some classic career situations: if one describes you… gear up your urgency.

YOUNG EXECUTIVES AT A CAREER CROSSROADS

These executives are typically 28-46 years old, B.A./B.S. or M.B.A., doing well financially, either highly marketable and confident… or concerned because they have been blocked for some time.

Many of these people are at an important crossroad. And, many potentially great careers are lost at this critical stage. Some, of course, are highly marketable. It's important for these executives to explore *all* their options when making a move… not just one or two… and we'll surface these for you.

On the other hand, some executives are less confident. Some fail to discover the importance of broadening out before it's too late. Age can be a factor here. They're well aware of the bottlenecks that may prevent their growth where they are.

Some are in situations where they have not attracted attention from top management. Other talented people may be just ahead of them—or they may not be aligned well enough politically. Because they value their careers so highly, a bad move at this stage can be tragic. They must make the right move. Here, one of the keys is to uncover and market their full range of assets and transferable skills.

If these people don't control their careers now, they may lose the advantage of their good beginnings. They must stage their careers and plan their futures. Others are facing a marketability decline.

These people are often wise to consider new environments in smaller and medium-sized firms, and in emerging industries—where they can receive greater responsibility.

Working in an entrepreneurial environment and combining it with large corporate experience can be an excellent platform for future moves. Or, it could be time for some to take a calculated risk to make a dramatic move up financially. They are ready to do their boss's job... and perhaps much better!

Our clients like this have often made the mistake of just dabbling in the market... answering ads, speaking with a few recruiters. The trouble is, that while they might have surfaced something sooner or later, it would only have been one offer—requiring a one-shot leap of faith.

For these people, having a structured system for developing the right interviews is critical. Good numbers are necessary because executives have to be realistic about rejections. And, the higher you go, the truer this is.

CORPORATE OFFICERS IN BAD CAREER POSITIONS

The corporate officer—$100K to $750K+... age 36 to 62... often at the peak of their marketability. Their job is threatened, the challenge is gone, or they have been terminated.

People in this position are often unsure about their futures. Normally in control, they sense changes ahead. A few may be concerned that they have wasted their best career opportunity.

Others may be fed up with politics and want out entirely. Some worry their careers could be lost.

At higher levels, these people are often concerned about campaigning with dignity. They also feel that they cannot afford to make another mistake. Their next move often needs to be their last. Time may be their greatest enemy.

There is a tendency for these professionals to have an exaggerated view of their marketability. Instead, they need to plan on getting much wider exposure than they may have realized.

Of course, for corporate officers at senior levels, the need for truly superior marketing materials is critical. That's what makes or breaks the success of these campaigns.

IF YOU HAVE HAD TOO MANY JOBS

Often, a client will come to us after several bad moves. Emotionally, they may be confused, and despite talent, they are doubting themselves.

Typically, this is where an executive is concerned and wondering if there is any hope. Is the problem with them, or are they a victim of circumstances?

In this situation, if you examine your previous changes, you'll probably see that bad moves in the past were made because you didn't professionally search. You took situations that just came your way.

At this stage, you need to control your career destiny. Mistakes must be avoided and a move made on a more scientific basis.

Historically, many have overreacted against past problems by taking the first thing that came along. For most people in this position, the key to success is in their ability to generate a lot of interviews. Then, you can be selective, accept the right situation and stay with it.

BEEN TOO LONG IN ONE FIRM OR INDUSTRY?

These people do not know what they are worth and may never have looked before. For this reason, the ability to expand their true marketability is paramount.

Unless their lethargy is shaken, these people may spend the best years of their lives with indecision. Action for these people may come too late to be meaningful.

Most of the time, these people are unaware of what's really out there for them.

Not only are they unaware of what's out there, but employers will be ignorant of their value, because they have never prepared materials to present their full story.

And whenever there's a problem of ignorance, the solution is communication.

If you are in this category, the weight of your campaign will fall on our ability to build an appropriate bridge, from where you've been—to where you want to be... both through your resumes and communication in general. We get concerned that in this category, the longer some wait, the more difficult the search may be.

ENTREPRENEURS ENTERING THE MARKET

These executives recognize that certain employers will be hesitant to hire them. They know there will be concerns about whether they may go back into their own business, whether they can be a team player in a corporate structure.

Talented as they may be, former entrepreneurs face special challenges. Many are identified with a narrow industry, and they lack credibility outside that niche. Of course, some want, or need by virtue of non-compete agreements, to seek out positions in different industries. However, they are unsure of where they would fit.

Some, having achieved success, want to be in a business that has an explicit mission of enriching people's lives.

If you are in this category, this is a critical move for you. You have not done this before, and you need to do it right. Chances are you are also a down-to-earth realist. To have credibility, you must have concrete "selling propositions," as well as "industry hooks" based on facts and the realities of the marketplace, not just vague generalities.

Entrepreneurs are seldom short on achievements. However, what you need are powerful written presentations that make you credible over a broader spectrum… and we will develop those for you.

WHEN YOUR AGE IS A POSSIBLE PROBLEM

Many people have doubts about competing. Their age may be a barrier for the responsibility their pride and ego demands. Regrettably, if they believe age is the barrier, and remain unhappily employed elsewhere, this mental obstacle blocks their putting forth the energy to make the right move.

Dealing with perceptions about age is like any other task. You progress if you take action. As you might suspect, action starts with your beliefs about yourself and what's possible. Barriers will fall as your marketable skills are surfaced.

You'll come to understand that your marketability can be enhanced through communication of all the skills, know-how and personal strengths you possess.

If you can contribute, age is irrelevant. Employers think about themselves, their problems and their own challenges. Of course, age will eliminate you from opportunities. That's why aggressiveness is called for… and you need to put the numbers on your side.

When we work with anyone concerned with age, we look to identify all the credible industry hooks they possess—broadening the functions they can fill, and the industries they can target.

NOW IS THE TIME TO PRIORITIZE YOUR GOALS

- Greater income
- More responsibility
- More recognition
- A better future
- New environment
- Enjoy work everyday
- Relocate
- Work with a leader
- Get into a new industry
- Travel less
- A new career
- Make new friends

3 Our next step is to help you expand your marketability beyond your factual credentials.

We pinpoint phrases describing your assets and transferable skills. These should be used consistently in all your communications, and will expand your marketability. We will also suggest ways to help neutralize any liabilities that might restrict your search.

ONE OF OUR GOALS WILL BE TO
EXPAND YOUR MARKETABILITY

Don't trap yourself by thinking you can say *"This is simply who I am, where I've been and what I've done."* People fail because they never communicate all that's marketable about themselves... and they never build their appeal beyond factual credentials.

Our starting point is to organize your lifetime of experiences. Whatever your level, there is probably much more to your story than meets the eye. Organizing past experiences and achievements reveals insights that can help us build your appeal.

Experience has proven that many people never identify 50% of what they should market. We've learned that most people need to identify 10 to 20 skills which, if properly communicated, can make a major difference in creating demand.

Each year, about 20% of the clients who come to us have settled for less, simply because they never communicated their real skills. For example, one client was earning a $65,000 base after 20 years. Three years later, she is earning $180,000. Another executive came to us at $125,000. Three years later, he is a CEO at many times that amount. The key in both situations was to market their true skills.

Now, if you are like most people, you can increase your chances through a very simple rule. It has been said by psychologists, spiritual leaders and coaches that the most restrictive limits you face are those you put on yourself. So, don't limit your thinking!

YOUR KNOWLEDGE, PERSONALITY & TRANSFERABLE SKILLS ARE MARKETABLE

Do you have knowledge of a product, a process or a market, from work, hobbies, relationships, research or suppliers? If so, it may be marketable.

Personality, of course, is just a word for that combination of traits that either attracts us to someone, or leaves us unimpressed. More employment decisions are based on personality and chemistry than any other factor.

For example: *"He's certainly professional and quick-thinking. I like him, and better yet, I trust him. He'll fit in with our team. I need to get him into the firm."* The perception of your personality has to do with your interest and enthusiasm. How many people get hired because they showed real interest? *A lot!*

Identifying transferable skills is critical. Today, employers place a premium on people who move through challenges, handling assignments that draw upon different skills. Your experience can also be reviewed by various "functions" such as sales, production, accounting, marketing and HR.

All areas in which you have knowledge must be identified. At the same time, you need to think of your experience in terms of "action words" that describe what you did... your achievements... i.e., *controlled, wrote, reshaped,* etc.

YOUR LEADERSHIP QUALITIES ARE MARKETABLE

If there is one quality you want to communicate, it is leadership ability. Leaders possess and communicate real convictions—strong feelings and principles that have grown with them over time. Leadership is also attributed to those who create an image of operating at the far edge of the frontier… into new products, new services and new solutions.

We expect leaders to have the vision and talent to develop new things. Another skill common to most leaders is their ability to assemble teams and to motivate them to peak achievement. Often creative, intuitive and passionate, they project integrity and trust. If you have these traits, they should be marketed. Image, attitude and presence also play a role.

The more ways we can describe your experience, the more we will qualify you for jobs in many industries. Our strategy will be to pinpoint and sell your transferable skills—the key to expanding your marketability beyond your factual credentials.

4 For many people, it's important for us to identify industry options to explore.

We use our extensive file of faster growing firms to isolate certain target industries—where your transferable skills will be well received. We also use our own software to isolate industries which match up with your prior experience.

IF APPROPRIATE, WE WILL JOINTLY DETERMINE THE RIGHT INDUSTRY OPTIONS FOR YOU

People of all ages are making moves into emerging industries. Many find such choices allow them to have greater income and more challenge. Here, we'll share some basics we've learned.

Transition to a new industry is easier than it used to be. Typically, people overrate the barriers and underrate their abilities to move into new areas. Today, most new jobs are created by small and mid-sized business units. So, you may want to explore positions with startups or emerging companies.

Choosing the right industry is important. When you do, you'll have growth opportunities, regular pay increases, meaningful stock options, positive environment and a longer term career. If you choose the wrong industry, chances are you will experience slower promotions, fewer raises, possible cutbacks, reduced compensation and sometimes forced early retirement.

Anyone who doesn't identify their industry options… and market transferable skills… will put very real limits on their career search.

There are ways we identify your new industry options. The first way is to identify the fastest growing industries and companies. These firms go outside their industry for the best talent and best skills.

The second way is to list characteristics of your industries… then find similar industries. Our software matches you up to new industries.

Keep in mind that projecting some form of an industry hook is the next best thing to having industry experience. When we compile a person's best possibilities, we often group them three ways:

(1) close industry hooks... easy possibilities;

(2) medium industry hooks... next best;

(3) far reach or stretch industry hooks.

If you are short on information about an industry, one way to acquire knowledge is by speaking with people in the industry or through trade publications. This makes it easy for you to talk about new products, specific firms and industry challenges. Our research staff can be a big help here.

Executives who have worked for firms under pressure can be invaluable contributors. Tough lessons learned in competitive battles can put you in demand in new industries.

Also, while glamorous high-tech and service businesses receive 90% of all publicity, many people find more opportunities in industries that are considered low-tech... or who have problems.

When changing industries, you also don't want to overlook your leverage power... the added benefits you may bring by virtue of your contacts or knowledge.

You may be able to bring a team with you that helped you "turn around" a similar situation. Perhaps you control major accounts. Or, you may have cut costs and can do it again.

5 We will professionally write all your resumes... and all your marketing letters.

Our staff will professionally write your universal, electronic and quick response resumes. Our goal is to capture the best expression of your experiences and skills plus your ability to contribute at the next level. We will also professionally draft any letters you might require.

WE WILL WRITE YOUR
RESUMES & LETTERS FOR YOU

The growth of PCs, faxes, the Internet and email has resulted in firms receiving *50 times* more resumes. Employers and recruiters have shifted to resume-scanning and database driven selection processes.

ITS, as a result of tracking thousands of searches, has developed a more effective approach—one which uses several resumes for different applications.

Your universal resume

The first resume we do is a universal resume—a one-page document that will be your introductory resume. Most people mistakenly believe that they need to tell their whole story in a resume. The reality is that you get better results when your initial resume is interesting, with a feeling of action—but short!

Your electronic or "Internet" resume

It is surprising how few devote any thought to the way their resumes appear at the receiving end of an email transmission. This 2nd resume will be shorter and to the point. When you are online, less is more. All you want is a response.

Your "quick-response" resume

This is the third resume we will do for you. It's a resume that makes it easy for you to respond quickly to certain emerging situations you discover. It positions the text on the right-hand side so that you can write notes on it instead of using a cover letter.

An optional resume—an "interview" resume

An interview resume intentionally reveals more. It is for presenting after your interviews when employers want to know more about you. Since it reveals more about your industry experiences, it could hurt your response if used initially. However, once you've been interviewed, this can be a compelling document.

An optional resume—an executive biography

This can be extremely powerful. It is essential for C-level jobs, and for those who will be hired with the approval of the president. Most people seeking $200,000+ should have this resume.

Senior decision makers often pass on a resume to get consensus. The offer depends on a "thumbs up" from the presentation. A 3 to 5 page resume, a bio is written in a narrative style and from a third-party perspective. It uses long stories, rich in detail, and is favored by top recruiters. Many of our clients find that this resume is very effective when networking... and when submitted during negotiations.

Our biographies have often been praised by prestigious recruiters because it makes it easier for them to sell a candidate to their corporate clients.

You should feel every resume you send out has some "WOW" potential. Multiple resumes can lift response by 300%. Our resumes are designed to "presell you," have people look forward to meeting you and reduce your interviewing pressure.

Our creative review board process

Each resume we prepare goes through 3 or 4 drafts... and must be presented to the firm's regional or national creative review board. Other veteran staff members offer their analysis of your documents. Only after this procedure are our materials ready for presentation to you.

The letters we create

We also professionally write any letters you may require. Here are the typical letters that we create for most people.

- ❏   For responding to openings
- ❏   For contacting recruiters
- ❏   For contacting venture capitalists
- ❏   For responding to spot opportunities
- ❏   For direct mail contact with employers
- ❏   For sponsored direct mail to employers
- ❏   For contacting directors of associations
- ❏   For networking associates and friends
- ❏   For networking alumni
- ❏   For networking influential people
- ❏   For setting up potential references
- ❏   For following up your interviews

TWO SUBSIDIARIES, JMAC... AND EMS... WILL ALSO SERVE YOU.

JMAC, our Job Market Access Center, is our technology company that specializes in meeting your information needs. This includes putting openings at your fingertips... delivering leads to you... and getting any research and information request quickly delivered to you.

EMS, which stands for Executive Mailing Service, is our distribution subsidiary. They have a separate specialty which involves managing the placement of your credentials with recruiters, growth firms, key employers... and sometimes venture capitalists.

The following pages will discuss the services that they will be providing as you go through your search.

6 Through JMAC, we will enable you to access the openings you need.

Through our subsidiary, JMAC, you have instant access to approximately 2 million openings. You simply click on boxes like those shown below.

3,000	2,100	1,500	3,500	100,000
Newspapers	Trade Mag's	Job Boards	Recruiters	Employers

WE WILL CONTINUOUSLY SUPPLY OPENINGS FOR YOU

What would it mean to you... if you had access to all the right openings... and all in the right place? This is what one of our subsidiaries... JMAC... can now do for you... locally, regionally or on a national basis.

This means that when you search for a new position, you can learn about 85% of what's out there for you... instead of the 2% you might uncover on your own.

Through JMAC worldwide, we provide instant access to virtually all openings in the published job market... and all openings on the Internet. If you've tried to find a lot of the right openings for yourself, you know it's not easy, and on your own it takes a lot of time.

At the bottom of the left-hand page, you will see five buttons. Behind each is a search engine for finding openings through the channels as indicated. This makes continuous openings available immediately at the touch of a button.

For example, through the first three buttons on the left... you can quickly get to openings in any of 3,000 newspapers... 2,100 trade magazines... and more than 1,500 job boards. Through our fourth button... 3,500 recruiters... you can review openings with recruiters in any location. If you respond to a specific situation they are working on right now... then your materials will be given an extra close look.

The fifth button... 100,000 employers... lets you instantly view the openings employers have on their websites... in your metro area... and industries of interest. Hiring this way is the biggest trend in recruiting... because it's much less expensive for employers.

The firm has also developed some special software called Advertised Market Supersearch. Through this software, we allow you to simultaneously search openings from up to 600 sources at one time, and get a response in seconds.

When you are accessing openings, you can also expand the situations you can respond to through upgrading or downgrading ads. For example, a company advertising a VP position may be willing to hire an Assistant VP or Director, who could move up to VP in a year. After all, it isn't so much the title they are after as the skills and talent. That's ***downgrading.***

By the same token, a firm advertising for a Plant Manager might be persuaded to hire a VP of Manufacturing, if someone could persuade them such a move would be cost efficient and give added capabilities. That's an ***upgrade.***

Did you ever see an ad and feel "that describes me exactly"? Well, you should follow up on every ad for which you are well qualified. Few of your competitors will do this.

You should also keep in mind that using letters alone and following up can help your response rate.

Employers who must sift through many resumes tend to start by screening out non-qualifiers. And, since resumes provide more facts, they can sometimes work against you. For this reason, consider using a strong letter tailored to the requirements of the position.

Employers rare-
ly find the perfect
candidate. So, try
to compensate for
any shortfall on cre-
dentials through an
expression of enthu-
siasm, or by explain-
ing why you might be
qualified. Whatever
your basis for selecting an advertisement, let the
employer know why you selected it.

You may also wish to try some creative responses
when answering openings. For example, you could
get additional information, beyond what was in the
ad, and use it in your response. You can do this by
reviewing product literature, websites, annual reports
or articles. Demonstrating industry knowledge works
better than anything else.

Another technique is to develop third party contacts with employees before responding. Easiest to
befriend are sales and marketing managers. Then, you
can mention their names in your correspondence.

As you respond to situations, you should also
be aware of the privacy issues that have developed
along with the Internet. Most firms sell access to
their database of resumes to employers looking for
candidates. Since many words in your resume are
scannable, someone who uses their services might
uncover your resume. This is one more reason for
using short resumes, materials that don't reveal
anything unnecessary.

7 Through JMAC, we will continuously supply you with leads to emerging situations.

Our Marketing Directors set "search agents" for you to automatically deliver relevant leads from news stories. These leads can be a critical factor in allowing you to compete in the unpublished job market.

WE WILL CONTINUOUSLY SUPPLY "LEADS" TO YOU

What would it mean to you... if besides having openings... you could get leads to emerging situations... jobs which have yet to be thrown open to the public?

Some remarkable new technology now allows us to put at your fingertips... leads to emerging opportunities... and in the industries and metro areas that interest you.

Where do we get these leads? Thousands of them come to us every day, from the major wire services... Associated Press, UPI and others. They're all about breaking business news... company expansions... firms relocating to your community... and many other "unfolding events."

These are proven leads to new jobs in the earliest stages... allowing you to get in the door first and avoid competition. They are "streamed" to you daily... by the industries you prefer... and by metro areas of interest.

We set search agents that filter out everything that's not of interest... so you can zero in on the locations and industries that appeal to you. These leads feed directly to your email every day. You will become the "ultimate insider" for the locations and industries you specify. No one will know more about "what's happening" inside key employers and organizations.

The JMAC division of ITS is the first firm in the world to develop software that makes this possible. There is simply no way... any individual on his or her own... can possibly surface all these leads on a regular basis.

As you go up the income scale, where published openings are more scarce, being able to access these leads becomes very important. In fact, without access to these leads, the typical person will miss out on hundreds of developing opportunities in their geographic area.

For companies undergoing these transitions, chances are they will need to attract good people to handle problems or capitalize on opportunities.

Their activities won't just be limited to one or two functions. They can be expected to need people in all functional categories: sales, marketing, finance, etc. What's more, when you connect with these situations, they will generally be much less competitive than when competing for published openings.

You also want to be sure not to ignore leads to troubled employers. Leads to reorganizations signal shifts within the executive ranks. They usually spell opportunity for those at the next lower level, and then changes ripple through the organization down the line.

Problems often imply one of two things: managers in certain functions haven't been performing well, or the company needs to develop new capabilities in order to survive and grow. Organizations with problems often need help from a wide range of people.

HOW THE JOB
MARKET IS FORMED

Some event occurs

- People are separated
- People resign... or retire
- Firms get capital
- New businesses are started
- Major contracts are awarded
- Record profits lead to expansion
- New products are created
- Firms relocate

Jobs are planned for

These events cause executives to think about hiring new staff.

As jobs are released and decisions are made... the job market is formed.

Jobs become available in one of these segments

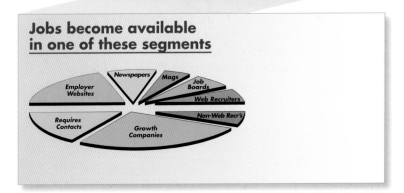

HOW SOME OF OUR CLIENTS MADE LEADS WORK

"I saw that a group of CPAs had formed a new firm here in Kansas City, which was near my home. Less than three weeks after contacting, I started my new job in accounting."

"I read that a troubled manufacturer was divesting a division to raise cash. I called the new president. Four weeks later, I became CFO."

"My previous job was as a GM. I read that a major investment was being made near my home. I got through after three attempts to the CEO and in one month was offered a position."

"I wanted to work in the sports marketing field and saw a lead about a partnership investment of a top basketball player. It took me a number of calls, but now I'm where I wanted to be."

"I had felt that age would be a big problem. With the story and materials ITS developed with your lead program, I had all the interviews I needed."

As a former CFO I knew I could help companies in trouble. So, using the lead program was my primary focus. I live in Central Florida and developed several offers approaching 200K."

"I had been in customer service and wanted a chance in sales. When a nearby firm was acquired, I sent a letter to the top sales executive at the acquiring firm. Several weeks later, I had the job I wanted."

"I had been in my own legal practice for 25 years. I saw that a major auto firm was investing in our area of Alabama. I got an audience with their General Counsel who brought me in as their legal liaison with headquarters."

"I was an administrator of a university hospital. One of your leads was about a medical equipment firm and I soon started in a position with 20% higher income."

"I wanted to get into consulting, but did not feel it was possible because of my age. When I saw that a new office of a prestige firm was being established, I got my opportunity."

8 Through EMS, we will place your credentials with your highest probability prospects.

We market you on a direct basis to local growth firms, key employers, recruiters and VCs. Typically, we place your credentials with thousands of organizations and decision makers... who represent your highest probability prospects.

WE PLACE YOUR CREDENTIALS WITH EMPLOYERS

If we were able to place your materials with all of your best prospects... in the area where you wanted to live... what do you expect it will mean for you?

Accomplishing this is not an exact science... but it is what we try to do for all of our clients. And, this is one of the fastest ways to compete for the openings which are unpublished.

We've learned it pays to aggressively contact key decision makers at companies which are good prospects for you. For this reason, as mentioned, we have formed a separate ITS division, Executive Mailing Service, or EMS... that distributes your credentials... and does much of the hard part of job hunting.

For example, for most professionals... we place their materials with thousands of key recruiters, key employers, growth firms... and perhaps venture capitalists.

The reason for contacting so many, is that when you use direct mail, fax or email... you only get a small response. You have to realize that a very low percentage will need someone like you the day your material arrives. But, the people who respond will want to see you. These can be your best qualified opportunities.

For many people... contacting employers in large numbers... can be an extremely fast way to get a lot of interviews.

With large distributions into the thousands, people often get 10 to 25 employers interested in seeing them. Other more highly marketable people can attract even greater interest... and 30 to 40 emails and calls are not unusual.

For the average job seeker, this is the part of job hunting that stops them. The task of handling thousands of distributions is simply too overwhelming. So, unfortunately, they miss out on many attractive jobs that are unpublished.

Of course, to make a direct approach work, you need to have excellent materials. I asked a friend of mine, a top recruiter, how important it was to have the right materials. His response was, *"I get a lot of resumes, but if the person really comes across well, I call them within days. The whole key is to have great materials."* Another, a VP of Marketing said, *"Recruiting professionals is expensive. It's hard work and takes a lot of time. A great resume makes my job easier and saves us time and money."*

When you approach companies on a direct basis, it's important to select the right targets... focusing on smaller or medium-sized firms usually produces the best results.

Many people tend to have *"tunnel vision"* and are handicapped because they restricting themselves to one or two industries. To build broader appeal, we need to market your transferable skills. So, as we develop your resumes, we focus on these factors. Then, we compile a broad list of organizations—your highest probability targets.

You also need to keep in mind that going direct to employers works best with smaller and mid-sized firms. Their officers tend to make hiring decisions more quickly.

On the other hand, in larger organizations, multiple contacts with different executives in the same company can work very well. With large companies the competition is more intense, so getting to "the right person" with "the right message" is even more critical.

The single most important thing in job hunting is to have a lot of people call you... and get a lot of interviews. From a negotiation standpoint, you also need to be aggressive enough so that you can have interviews maturing into several offers at the same time.

Another advantage is that going direct can produce leads in a less competitive situation. In addition, keep in mind that situations which seem to be of little interest, can be upgraded in the same firm or networked to other opportunities.

9 **Through EMS, we will place your credentials with many recruiters—simultaneously.**

We will market you to all appropriate local recruiters... and we can market you to national recruiters, as well.

WE WILL PLACE YOUR CREDENTIALS WITH RECRUITERS

Whether they are called search firms or headhunters, all recruiters work for employers. Their function is to locate, screen and recommend prospective employees. These firms *are not* in business to serve job hunters. They fill jobs at $60,000 to $1,000,000 and up. Typically, they are retained for exclusive searches at fees averaging up to 33% of compensation.

To distinguish themselves, executive search firms are referred to as "retained recruiters." Other firms, contingency recruiters, are active up to $150,000, but receive a commission only when a placement is made.

Another growing category is the "temporary or contract recruiter." They earn fees when employers hire professionals on an interim basis.

While 8,000 firms claim to be active as executive recruiters, fewer than 30 dominate the upper-end business. Importantly, the best recruiters play a role in helping management set up position specifications.

Local and regional recruiters have been playing an increasingly important role in the job market. Some specialize by industry... and others by career fields. Today, there are thousands of local recruiters which can be helpful.

Recruiters are articulate professionals who have a broad knowledge of business, and who are excellent marketing executives themselves. It will pay you to develop relationships with those you respect and to maintain them throughout your career. They know what's going on in their local markets.

Recruiters prefer achievers, people making strong first impressions and who are employed. Being visible in your industry can be key. Being in a hot area can help. Of course, to develop a good level of activity with recruiters, you'll need superior materials.

When you communicate with recruiters, never be negative about your employer and never appear desperate. Also, keep in mind that recruiters are "assignment-oriented." They need to fill their active contracts or job listings. So, we send them your resume, or you register online, simply to get placed in their files.

Here's what you expect when you do distributions to recruiters:

- People with recognizable "tickets" do best (well-known schools, degrees, blue chip firms, etc.).
- Those in popular occupations do best. Some response is quick, but most come over months.
- Contacting recruiters is less effective for those in low demand specialties or career changers.

When responses come in and they engage you on the phone, be ready with your 30-second commercial. Also, keep in mind that you will be most popular with recruiters if you will explore attractive situations, but are not openly unhappy. Because timing is critical, luck can also play a role.

Remember, the chance of a recruiter filling a job that is right for you, at the moment you contact them, is small. That's why we need to contact a lot of recruiters for you.

WE CAN ALSO PLACE YOUR CREDENTIALS WITH VCs

We can place your credentials with all appropriate local venture capitalists... or national firms. Many VC firms have assumed an active role in recruiting for firms in which they have an ongoing investment. We track the leading 2,600 venture capital firms in the U.S. VCs are for those who have an interest in new start-ups and small-to-medium-sized growth firms.

People who will generate the most interest are executives who are candidates for "C" level positions or those who can direct a line function (VP Sales, etc.). Typically, they are in their 30s and 40s, have been with major firms and have advanced degrees. If your background is appropriate, our Marketing Directors will also market you to local venture capitalists.

10 We will work with you on our process for getting jobs created to fit your needs.

You can develop offers, even when no current openings exist. You simply need to present yourself as a solution to a problem or the key to an opportunity. In fact, the higher you go, the more likely your next position will be created for you.

WE WILL HELP YOU GET JOBS CREATED

The organizations most likely to create a job will include firms that are growing rapidly, bringing out new products, forming new divisions, acquiring other companies, or reorganizing. These are the firms that need good people, often from other industries, who make decisions quickly.

Your goal would be to communicate directly with the person you would most likely work for, or their boss. The key for you is to be able to communicate a suitable benefit proposition.

This should be a concise description of what you can do. You need to present the promise of value on a scale large enough to warrant an investment in you. In your initial communication, you must establish your credentials and mention past results. Achievements you cite don't have to be large, but they do have to be significant.

Dealing with opportunities is a key job for many executives. Most don't have enough time, and they are predisposed to positive news from people who can help them. They will want to believe your message.

Remember, when you go to the interview, you're going to have to address the benefits that your communication promised. You can expect questions such as: *What are your ideas? What makes you confident that they'll work?*

Do you really understand this company, its problems and its opportunities? Address these areas, but always remember to convey humility. Acknowledge that the other person has a better grasp of the problems than you could possibly have.

One of your first goals is to find out how the employer views the problem. *What do they see as the key challenges? What is their "hot button"? Where are their priorities? What attempts have been made in the past?*

By asking a few questions and listening carefully, you will find out what the employer really wants. Ask questions and make positive comments in response to the interviewer's remarks. Try to get the employer to share his innermost thoughts—his vision for the firm. If you are able to accomplish this in the first interview, that's enough.

In your second interview, reinforce your value by drawing a picture of the benefits you can bring. Then, build enough enthusiasm to get an offer or be asked to speak with others.

Keep in mind that you will need to stir the employer's imagination. Your conversations should focus on the future. Convey enthusiasm and create a sense of excitement. Be ready to discuss approaches you would take to reinforce the notion that you will succeed.

If you build sufficient enthusiasm, the employer may conclude the meeting with a statement that they want to create a job for you.

Using "leads" we supply to find
emerging opportunities & to get a
job created... is a key strategy. The
higher your income, the more this is.

11 If you wish to network, our staff will supply an approach that works.

Through JMAC you can uncover old contacts you may have lost track of. We can also fulfill any information requests you may have… e.g., for names of executives in industries who may be high probability networking possibilities.

WITH SUPERIOR MATERIALS & THE RIGHT INDUSTRY FOCUS
NETWORKING CAN WORK

We recommend you focus your networking on industries which have characteristics that make you a good match.

Seeking *informational interviews* is the most popular networking approach. Here, you wish to encourage executives to share with you information about their industry, trends and challenges. These discussions must be kept brief, and you need to have your list of questions prepared. As a rule, people do better when they have researched a firm and ask for feedback on ideas that may benefit the firm.

Executives to target should be influential people. Consider looking for those who have been featured in articles, which makes an introduction easy and natural. Also be sure to track down lost contacts, uncover successful alumni and others. Executive Directors of associations have "lines" into industries. Editors of business magazines and newsletters often have an inside track on company needs.

We all have friends who have influential friends… golfing partners, politicians, lawyers, investment bankers, etc., who know others who could be looking for someone like you. All they need to do is handwrite a short note and forward your materials.

NETWORKING REFERENCES

Mark was a VP who wanted to become a CFO. We helped make Mark aware of the power of his references. When Mark heard his company was to be sold, he felt his salary was $20,000 less than it should be.

Did his boss feel bad about paying him less? Absolutely! Could Mark ask him to act as a reference, and would he raise him to the level he wanted, in return for staying for the last two months? Definitely.

Now, the boss had a friend in an accounting firm. Mark asked his boss if he would approach his friend as a second reference. Together, they had lunch. The accountant was happy to be a second reference. In the same way, Mark developed a third reference, his own brother-in-law.

When he launched a campaign, he had a good interview with the president of a small company. A conservative man, he asked for three references. Mark immediately recontacted his references, so they were ready. After his boss had given him a glowing reference, the president mentioned he was still uncertain.

When the second reference was called (the boss's friend), he told the president that in the right situation Mark could help save $1 million in taxes, and control costs. He had repositioned Mark as a broader-based financial executive.

Next, Mark's third reference supported the others and added a few points. The day after the last reference check, he got a call from the president, and guess what? His message was, *"Mark, what will it take to get you?"* He ended up as CFO at a much higher income.

Most of the time, important references will be the people you reported to in the past, or the person you currently report to or their superiors. Choose the highest level reference, as long as you get an enthusiastic endorsement, and avoid people who don't communicate well. Also be sure to give them an idea of what to emphasize about your background.

SELECTING REFERENCES

References you select should know your achievements and have no hesitation in making strong statements. What they say is very important, but the enthusiasm they project is more important. Let them know that you have high regard for them and their opinions, and they will want to do their very best.

Also, make sure that your references know the full story. Here's an example. A woman who worked for me left to complete her MBA. She was competent, had a quiet manner, but could be forceful. When she started interviewing, she brought me up-to-date. She called after an interview to tell me that she felt they had some concerns about her quiet nature.

Armed with that information, I was ready when I was called by her potential boss. Before the question was asked, I mentioned that sometimes people could be deceived by this woman's quiet nature, but that she could be very assertive. The person responded that I had put to rest his one concern.

References can be your best sources of referrals. Leave each person a half-dozen resumes. Reassure them that you won't use them too many times. After calling them, send a brief note that shows your appreciation and summarize a few positive things they can say about you. You can even make a list of questions that employers might ask and suggest answers for them.

By the way, let references know as soon as you have used their names, and ask them to let you know when they have been contacted. Employers will often ask them for the name of someone else who is familiar with you.

If someone is apt to give you a bad reference, you need to bring it out in the interview and supply enough good ones to offset it.

For example, if the interviewer asks to speak with a reference who will be questionable, defuse the situation by explaining that you had differences of opinion on some managerial styles. Remain objective and unemotional, and never imply negatives.

Also, if you are doubtful about what a reference might say, you might have a friend do a mock reference check to find out what is being said. If the reference is neutral, don't hesitate to ask the person to furnish more positive information. If necessary, explain that any negative input is keeping you from winning a position and enabling you to support yourself.

12 How we will be assisting you throughout your interviews.

You may not have interviewed in years... or... you may not have ever interviewed at the income level you are now seeking. Regardless of your situation, we want to make sure that you convert a good percentage of your interviews into offers.

THE INTERVIEWING GOALS WE HELP YOU WITH

1. Read the interviewer's personality.

2. Maximize personal chemistry.

3. Tell memorable stories.

4. Know what questions to ask.

5. Know about the employer.

6. Be able to answer difficult questions.

HOW WE HELP CONVERT YOUR INTERVIEWS INTO OFFERS

Let's briefly review some things that will help you come out better than your competition.

Have you ever had a "perfect" interview... and then never heard back? Well, at ITS we've met a lot of top executives who had fallen flat when it came to interviews. It's because interviewing is no different from other skills. How good would you be if you only played golf or tennis... once in a while?

Let's take an example. Let's assume you had good interviews and a company calls you back for a final meeting... but they add that they are bringing in five other finalists... and a decision will be made shortly.

Would you know what to do... and how to approach this type of situation? As our client, we want you prepared to do the following.

■ We would like you to be able to read the interviewer's personality and adjust your behavior accordingly.

■ We want you to know how to maximize personal chemistry. When you get right down to it... people hire people they like.

■ We want you to tell memorable stories. People like stories and remember them.

■ We want you to know what questions to ask. That allows you to control the pace of these discussions.

■ We want you to always know as much as you can about the employer. Companies prefer candidates who have taken the time to know about them. (This is where our research staff comes in... as they can get you information before interviews.)

■ We would like you to know how to answer difficult questions.

An ITS client who was the top HR executive at CitiGroup, told us that he was amazed... but that when it comes to hard questions... *"a lot of top executives fumble away their best opportunities."*

So, to help here... the ITS staff will supply a list of difficult questions people might face... and we will assist you in developing seamless and very smooth responses.

Without taking advantage of our assistance, you might work hard at developing the good interviews... only to continually lose out to others in competitive situations.

With support from a team of our specialists, you'll never be out there alone. You get help with any issue, concern or question.

13 How we will be assisting you throughout your negotiations.

Every week, our staff is involved with dozens of negotiations, and we play a key role with our clients during this stage.

OUR 4 NEGOTIATION GOALS

1. Get your initial offers raised.

2. Expand the responsibilities of the job.

3. Possibly negotiate a signing bonus.

4. Negotiate benefits and stock options.

THE IMPORTANT BASICS
THE KEYS TO NEGOTIATING

With the right approach... people can often secure packages that are beyond what they ever thought possible. It may surprise you... but one of the most common mistakes people make... is to set their sights too low.

First, you need to consider what the right new job is worth to you. Negotiating more "now"... can turn into a substantial amount of total earnings... over the course of your career.

Essentially, if you leave $20,000 on the bargaining table... your failure will probably cost you at least $20,000... x 10... or $200,000. That's because chances are that whatever new income you start at... you will maintain that difference over where you were for the better part of your career.

There are many things that you might be able to negotiate... but most job seekers fail to bring them up. Unfortunately, when it comes to compensation, things have gotten much more complex.

To best appreciate what negotiation is about, let's assume a firm called you back after several interviews... and said they would have an offer for you.

Certainly, the firm would extend a good base salary... and would also make available their medical benefits. However, companies don't automatically give people other perks... you have to negotiate them. The problem is, that if you ask for too much... or in the wrong tone... you could jeopardize the offer.

The range of perks that might be available has gotten very complex... and you'll have a lot at stake.

At the core of all negotiations is a simple rule we follow at ITS. Never negotiate based on where you've been. The art of negotiating involves determining what the position is worth to the employer... and then to negotiate using a simple soft sell approach.

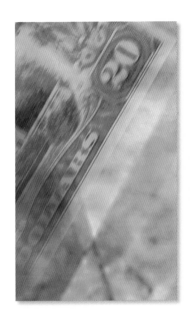

There are four key factors that you should try to accomplish in all your negotiations. The first we'll show you is knowing how to get an offer raised to a higher offer. Once you've gotten an offer, did you know it can often be raised by 10% to 30%? It might surprise you, but people do this all the time... and at all income levels.

The second factor has to do with knowing how to discuss the offer of a specific job... and get it redefined into a larger job... one that's worth more.

The third factor has to do with signing bonuses. But what you may not know is... that it's not just NFL quarterbacks and other star athletes who get them. Firms ranging from Merrill Lynch... to the U.S. government... will give out signing bonuses selectively... when it is to their recruiting advantage.

The fourth factor involves benefits and stock options. Here, you can be getting into the most complex form of negotiations... one that you may be unfamiliar with. At ITS, our approach is to use specialists to work with you on all your offers. Just by helping plan each written or verbal response during negotiations, we have found we can often save people tens of thousands of dollars and more.

14 If you are unemployed... it's important to turn your situation to your advantage.

When you are unemployed, your advantage is your time, and your ability to get going on an aggressive scale. Here are seven key steps if you become unemployed.

IF YOU ARE UNEMPLOYED
USE YOUR TIME TO TURN
IT INTO AN ADVANTAGE

As a group, virtually everyone who becomes unemployed becomes reemployed, but some do it quickly, while others settle for poor positions. Experience has shown that as time passes, the less psychologically capable you will be... to do what must be done to win a new job. So, the key is to have a schedule of full activity: breakfast and lunch meetings, interviews, letter writing, phone calls, follow-ups, and negotiations.

For action oriented people, being unemployed simply means having the time to do these things. First, see if you can get support from your employer. Many firms are concerned about the people they terminate and want to provide as much support as they can.

■ With respect to severance, firms will sometimes extend financial support.

■ Some will extend outplacement help.

■ Make sure there is agreement on why you were separated. Work out an explanation which puts you in the best light.

■ Be prepared to explain why you are unemployed. You can state that the termination was due to outside factors... such as a cutback, merger, or reorganization.

■ You can point out that the firm provided a generous severance to show appreciation.

■ Where it applies, make the point that the final separation was made at your initiative because you are a loyal person who gives 100% and you did not want to look for a job while drawing a paycheck.

- Be ready to provide references who will speak enthusiastically, not only about your performance, but your character and personality as well.

- Don't make the mistake of implying threats. If you are in a position to harm your employer, they will know about it, and they'll take it into account when they deal with you. It is to your advantage that your relationship remain positive.

- If you are terminated for performance, remind your employer that judgments about performance can be subjective, and point out that you could be seriously harmed by a negative reference.

Second, make sure you build your knowledge every day. And, be sure to share your progress with your Marketing Director.

Third, set aside one hour each morning to make a list of leads, ideas, and potential people to contact. Look for leads about any industry in which you are interested. Make it a rule to select three new people or companies to contact each day. Also, we suggest you devote two hours a day to sending out letters or phone calls based on your plan of action, and work to arrange at least one interview or personal meeting.

You also need to allow at least a half-hour each day for exercise. Positive thoughts come more easily to people who stay physically fit. If you will follow these simple ideas, you can be way ahead of most others who go through this experience.

10 COMMON PITFALLS WHEN UNEMPLOYED

■ **Turning down a first offer.** Even if it is not everything you hoped for, if it offers challenge and growth, it should be given careful consideration.

■ **No skepticism of the first offer.** This is the reverse of the last point. If a position is obviously not right for you, if it presents little challenge, or allows limited personal growth, then say "no thank you."

■ **Unwilling to relocate.** Sometimes it is better to go where new firms and industries are.

■ **Not accepting introductions.** We've all heard it. "I'm not going to press myself on my friends." The truth is, most people want to help friends.

■ **Feeling sorry.** It is a normal reaction, but, who is being hurt by these emotions? You are.

■ **Unrealistic income goals.** Instead of doing this, consider a two step move.

■ **Not considering a career change.** If your occupation is on the decline, consider something new.

■ **Allowing your health to slip.** Attitude and physical fitness go hand in hand.

■ **Allowing financial pressure to cause inertia.** Financial pressures are tough to withstand. Don't be afraid to borrow, or to take part-time work.

■ **Displaying a bad mood.** There are many outlets for stress, including physical fitness. Besides, a bad mood will alienate those trying to help you.

15 Your motivation counts a lot. Why not build an unstoppable will to succeed?

All members of our team will initiate calls to you on a frequent basis. Helping you maintain a positive attitude is important. Besides expertise, our team will supply direction, careful listening, encouragement and emotional support.

EVERYONE LIKES POSITIVE PEOPLE
THEY GET MORE OFFERS

A positive attitude is the most common thread among all winners. It will separate you from the many who give up or settle for less. It's easy to build a will to succeed if you follow six basic guidelines.

1. Develop positive beliefs

Remind yourself of all the good things you have done. Write down positive things "you've done and can do." Make it as long and complete as possible. You will find it reassuring. It will begin to provide reinforcement for the positive attitude you must maintain. All you need are short sentences.

For example: I have increased profits. I have attracted new business. I have cut costs, etc. Here are some "can do's" to consider: I can work with all levels of people. I can get things done quickly. I can motivate others, etc. They also reflect your *skill sets*. As you do this, you will begin to realize just what value you will have for your next employer.

2. Get rid of negative beliefs

Are you saying, "things are bad, it's a grim world out there." If so, this simply reflects your beliefs about "the way you think things really are." If you believe the economy is bad, you will see breaking news and pay attention to layoffs or sales declines. On the other hand, if you believe that there are many areas of opportunity, then you will notice new firms, new products and the like.

3. Set your expectations high

Our expectations have a lot to do with what happens for us. Obvious examples are the many sports teams and athletes who, when asked about their success, often reply, *"We expected all along that we would win."*

A close look at the lives of leaders in almost any field reveals a common theme. Whether it's a leading scientist, educator, salesperson, movie personality, or leader of industry, you'll find that each of them had very positive expectations of themselves.

All motivational speakers and inspirational leaders tell us that it is possible to work on our expectations by visualizing good things happening to us. Picture yourself setting and achieving high goals. Positive visualizations become a continuous process of reinforcement that will give you a new-found power.

4. Put positive expectations to work

For instance, if someone tells you that an interview can take only 15 minutes, recognize it's a screening interview and build expectations that it will allow you to showcase your potential.

Let's take another example. Suppose you had an excellent interview, called twice afterwards, and got no response. Don't assume they have lost interest. Instead, assume they're busy, and that they are still very interested. Decide now, that your second meeting will be better than the first. With that kind of expectation, you will then find it easy to write a short follow-up note that your interest continues to grow, and that you are dedicated to becoming the best ever in the job. Your expectations affect your actions and the results.

5. Project a positive attitude

You have put yourself on the line. Let your ideas flow into your general attitude, and begin to reach out and help others. Why? Once again, experts tell us this is a give and get world. Eventually, it reaches the point where it becomes obvious to anyone who meets you, that you project a lot of confidence.

You'll have to work at this, but it's easy and it's fun. A spring in your step, a firm handshake, a confident look in your eye, and comments which reveal a positive outlook can all help you project good feelings.

6. Make things happen

If you look at achievers in any field, you will find that they are very active people. It's a simple fact that taking action is in itself like taking an energy tonic.

Choose any kind of example you like. The head of a college breathing new life into an institution, a company president turning around a money losing operation, a football coach turning a losing team into winners, a home run hitter in the act of swinging the bat, or a test pilot setting a new speed record. They are so intent on their actions, there is no room for doubt and indecision. You can do the same thing.

Optimism and a positive attitude have a major impact on you... and everyone you meet. It's contagious!

ITS YOUR ITS GUARANTEES

We back every step of our service with the strongest possible guarantees.

For anyone we accept as a client, this eliminates uncertainty... placing any risk on us and how we perform for you.

(1) A money back guarantee on all resumes we create.

(2) An ongoing satisfaction guarantee regarding everything we present.

(3) A performance guarantee... if you don't get a suitable job in 90 to 120 days.

We provide these to make sure that you are totally comfortable using our services.

For any person we accept as a client for the ITS service... we provide the following strong guarantees.

■ **Our money back guarantee.** Upon presentation of your resumes, you must be fully satisfied that we have captured the very best expression of your credentials, transferable skills and ability to contribute... or we will immediately refund any retainers.

(Note: Over 98% of our clients tell us the resumes we create more than exceed their expectations. However, we extend this policy to clients worldwide to make every one of our clients feel totally comfortable with our firm.)

■ **Our satisfaction guarantee.** As you go through your search, you have to be satisfied with every stage of our work... or we redo it. In the rare event that you are dissatisfied, we do request that you promptly notify us upon presentation, so we can correct the situation.

■ **Here's how our performance guarantee works.** If you haven't succeeded within 90 to 120 days or are not closing in on a very good situation, we stand ready to do the following upon request.

First, we will assign a new marketing team and will develop a new marketing plan. **Second,** we underwrite the cost of rewriting any resumes and letters as needed. **Third,** we will re-implement all distributions that are part of our local marketing package. This has been necessary with less than 1% of all clients we have ever worked for.

ITS YOUR ITS ALUMNI BENEFITS

Once you've landed your new job, you'll automatically be registered in our "alumni" program... for the following benefits.

Here's what you get... for you and your family... for the next 5 years.

■ You can have a free professional career assessment for 5 years (once annually). Here, you get the benefit of evaluating your career situation and future prospects in-depth, with one of our seasoned professionals.

■ You have free online access to JMAC for you and your family (spouse and children) for 5 years.

ITS QUALITY CONTROL AT ITS

Retaining our service represents a serious commitment, and we want each client to have complete faith that they are engaging a firm with the highest standards. Our Board has dictated that we go to the greatest lengths to inform each candidate of all of our practices.

We do this through a policy known as full disclosure marketing. As part of it, we make available a wide variety of color materials on our system and our firm... along with a high content website and this client handbook that fully describes the service we provide and our philosophy.

To ensure that you are comfortable with us, our Board has also established the strongest consumer protection policies and guarantees in our field.

Our service standards, consumer protection policies, guarantees, and dispute resolution policies already far exceed any service in the employment field. We hold ourselves to the highest standards of accountability. In fact, our performance record is the envy of other firms in the employment field.

As you go through our service you will be asked to initial receipt of everything we have promised to do on your behalf. And, as you go through your search our service staff will be available daily to make sure that everything is running smoothly.

ITS THE ITS TRACK RECORD

In dealing with thousands of situations with the public, and human nature being what it is... some level of complaints is unavoidable. Nevertheless, with our full disclosure policy, and with the state-of-the-art service we provide, we have a remarkably high level of customer satisfaction.

Each month, tens of thousands of people have registered profiles with ITS — now averaging hundreds of thousands per year. In the course of 8 years more than 35,000 clients have been accepted. When problems occur, we deal with them instantly as part of our satisfaction guarantee... doing our work over to satisfy the client. Anything, no matter how minimal, is dealt with promptly. Our goal is 100% perfection.

But even with our effort, some situations cannot be resolved. In fact, from the clients served over an 8 year period... ending January 1, 2008, 140 clients... less than 16 per year... far less than 1%... remained disappointed, regardless of our initial efforts. When these occurred, our policy required that we make other aggressive efforts involving extra services and doing everything possible to resolve remaining complaints — even if we felt the requests were unreasonable.

To date, these extra efforts resulted in 87 of those clients having their situations resolved... leaving less than 1 in 853 (0.01%) feeling our service was not a good experience. On the other hand, tens of thousands have felt we've played a major role in changing their lives, improving their careers and putting them on a track for future growth.

ITS IS AVAILABLE BASED ON ACCEPTANCE ONLY

The ITS service is for the vast majority of individuals anywhere who feel they have a record of achievement at professional, managerial or executive levels. But, it is not for everyone.

Unfortunately, some start out with such a high degree of difficulty, that even with the immense leverage provided by our resources, it takes us too long to help move people into attractive positions in today's competitive environment. For this reason, our policy is to discourage certain people from using our service. For example:

- People who are not adequately motivated and do not meet our standards for commitment.

- People seeking relocation, but without a budget to travel to and from interviews.

- People with very narrow location needs outside of major metropolitan areas.

- Those with extreme specialization.

- Those with disabilities that prevent them from interviewing… or speaking easily.

- Those with poor educational credentials and limited achievements to compensate.

- Those with significant age issues and no record of contributions in demand today.

- And some who face bias due to personality, appearance, language or depression.

People in these categories need to consider that while our resources will enhance anyone's chances, their marketability does not allow us to take on their assignment.

ITS THE ITS PROMISE TO YOU

This guide is not just something that we ask you to read and understand for your own benefit. It is also our commitment to you... and we will do everything for you as stated in this client handbook.

For that reason, we think you should review it... read it again... then visit our company website at www.itspersonalmarketing.com, and get a feeling for the experiences of other clients.

With best wishes for your success.

Few things in life are more important than finding the right new job. Here are some other key factors that will play a major role in your ultimate success.

BE CONFIDENT

Confidence is all about positive expectations for good things to happen. It's essential because it affects your willingness to commit your energy, time and resources in pursuit of your search.

HAVE PASSION & DRIVE

Passion and drive make a difference. It's all about the work ethic we all bring to the table. Bring the same energy to this effort that has made you successful in other endeavors.

BE COMMITTED

Your degree of commitment will be influenced by your goals. So, select goals that mean a lot to you... and the pursuit of them will keep you committed.

INVEST IN YOURSELF

There is no new product... and there is no new business... that can get started without some investment. The same holds true for your personal marketing campaign. Without it, you run the risk of never getting off the ground.

TAKE INITIATIVES

One of the nice things about having access to our resources... is that you can get creative and very easily take many personal marketing actions you've never done before.

EXPECT TO WIN

In the end... with our system and all of our resources at your disposal, it will all come back to confidence. Make succeeding a self-fulfilling prophecy.

7979 E. Tufts Avenue Parkway, Suite 1400
Denver, CO 80237
1-866-328-2685

www.itspersonalmarketing.com